Allosaurus

Written by Ron Wilson
Illustrated by Doreen Edwards

Library of Congress Cataloging in Publication Data

Wilson, Ron, 1941-
Allosaurus.

Summary: Describes the meat-eating dinosaur, the allosaurus, and follows an elderly one in a search for food. Includes enrichment activities.
1. Allosaurus—Juvenile literature. [1. Allosaurus. 2. Dinosaurs] I. Title.
QE862.S3W54 1984 567.9'7 84-16097
ISBN 0-86592-206-3

Rourke Enterprises, Inc.
Vero Beach, FL 32964

Diplodocus
Pteranodon
Woolly Mammoth

Allosaurus

The old Allosaurus could not move as quickly as she used to. Finding food was not as easy as it had been in the past. There were also more of her own kind on the lookout for large creatures to kill and eat.

Wind and rain lashed the countryside. So heavy was the rain that the old Allosaurus had difficulty in seeing where she was going.

Suddenly the wind changed direction. As it did so, it increased in strength. The rain turned to hail. The large hailstones made the old dinosaur's eyes water. She held her head down.

At the onset of the storm most of the other creatures had taken shelter. The young Archaeopteryx had climbed into the nearest trees. Diplodocus had sought the shelter of a thicket.

The old Allosaurus was so hungry that she plodded on her way. She could not see where she was going. Head down to avoid the hailstones, she moved forward. She was stopped in her tracks as she walked headlong into a tree. Her massive form made the whole trunk tremble. Up in a fork of the tree an Archaeopteryx was disturbed and clung on tightly.

The storm was short-lived. The black clouds had gone, and in their place bright sunshine flooded the earth. The old Allosaurus felt better. Already other creatures had come out from their sheltering places. They were on the move again.

It was a long time since Allosaurus had had a good meal. She had taken some lizards and small mammals. However, these weren't enough to satisfy her hunger and keep her going.

Her belly ached from lack of food. The old creature looked around her. She saw a Diplodocus feeding in the distance. There was a Stegosaurus close by. She even noticed a Brontosaurus emerging from behind a large cycad.

The dinosaur paused for a moment. She knew from past experience that Diplodocus might be easier to attack than Brontosaurus. She certainly wanted to avoid the Stegosaurus.

She had made up her mind. Allosaurus moved off slowly at first, but as the pangs of hunger increased she hastened her steps just a little. Allosaurus saw the Diplodocus move away as it fed. Stegosaurus was now much nearer. Yet, Stegosaurus with its armor-plating would be more difficult to attack. The old Allosaurus realized that the creature would be too strong for her.

Allosaurus decided to leave the Stegosaurus to its food-hunting activities. She changed direction, hoping to approach the Diplodocus without being seen. There was plenty of cover from nearby trees and bushes. Allosaurus made for these.

She kept the Diplodocus in view. As she approached she caught sight of a Brontosaurus which was even closer. She changed course. The Brontosaurus was too busy browsing to notice. As Allosaurus trundled on she walked over several tree trunks which had fallen in the high winds. The sound of her feet crashing into them disturbed an Archaeopteryx. It let out a warning call. This was picked up by the other Archaeopteryx on the ground and in the trees.

Both Diplodocus and Brontosaurus heard the alarm cries. They looked up from their feeding. They both saw the Allosaurus approaching and made off in opposite directions.

Diplodocus moved off quickly. In her haste to avoid the approaching Allosaurus it had not seen another Allosaurus hiding behind a cycad. It was too late. Diplodocus tried to avoid it. Within seconds the Allosaurus had spotted Diplodocus. It moved forward ready for the kill. Diplodocus had no chance against this vicious creature. It struggled, but in spite of its great strength, its efforts were in vain. The Allosaurus had it firmly in its grip.

The old Allosaurus's hunger pangs were extremely great now. The smell of fresh flesh was too much to ignore. She continued to move towards the feeding Allosaurus and the dead Diplodocus.

She was still some way from the scene when the feeding Allosaurus let out a warning call. The old creature decided not to try her luck and turned away. As she did so she spotted an Archaeopteryx quietly feeding on insects close by.

There was little flesh on an Archaeopteryx, but anything would help to cure the hunger pangs. Allosaurus approached slowly. Within reach of Archaeopteryx it pounced. But the old creature was not quick enough. The bird escaped and climbed up the short trunk of a nearby tree.

Allosaurus went towards the tree. The old dinosaur put its front feet onto the trunk of the tree. Archaeopteryx was just out of reach. The frightened bird spread its wings and glided gently down to earth. It ran for cover as quickly as its legs would carry it.

Turning round the Allosaurus noticed that the Brontosaurus which it had spotted earlier was now feeding again. She decided to approach it. There was plenty of cover from the cycads. Allosaurus was very cautious. So great was her hunger that she must feed soon if she was to survive.

The Brontosaurus was feeding close to a tree. Allosaurus was making slow progress. She paused. Brontosaurus was almost within reach. Eager to get a meal, Allosaurus made a sudden lunge at the other dinosaur. She missed, and Brontosaurus ran off into the distance. As it went it bellowed a warning to the other creatures. They quickly scattered in all directions.

Allosaurus had little energy left. She sank to the ground with exhaustion. She was not sure whether she would be able to get up again. Food had been scarce for some time now. She had had to compete for it with the other more agile flesh-eaters. Now she was not sure what to do. Allosaurus rested for a while. Then she tried to get up. She couldn't make it. Already she had been spotted by other creatures eager for a meal.

A young Allosaurus approached. The old creature shouted a warning which meant 'stay away'. At the same time she tried again to get up. She managed to raise herself onto two feet, but sank back to the ground again.

Realizing that the old creature was not going to make it, the young Allosaurus pounced. It sank its clawed talons into the back of the weak Allosaurus. Huge fangs tore at the flesh. The old creature shrieked in pain. Within minutes another Allosaurus had arrived on the scene.

The old dinosaur was unable to fight, and within minutes she was dead. Quickly the two Allosaurus tore huge chunks of flesh from the body of the dead creature.

Several Ornitholestes had been hiding in bushes nearby. They had been waiting for such a moment. They dashed out, grabbed small pieces of meat in their jaws. They quickly ran back for cover. The Allosaurus were too busy to see them.

Soon there was little of the old Allosaurus left. Several large bones littered the ground as the well-fed younger Allosaurus ambled off into the distance, their hunger satisfied for another day.

Interesting facts about . . . Allosaurus

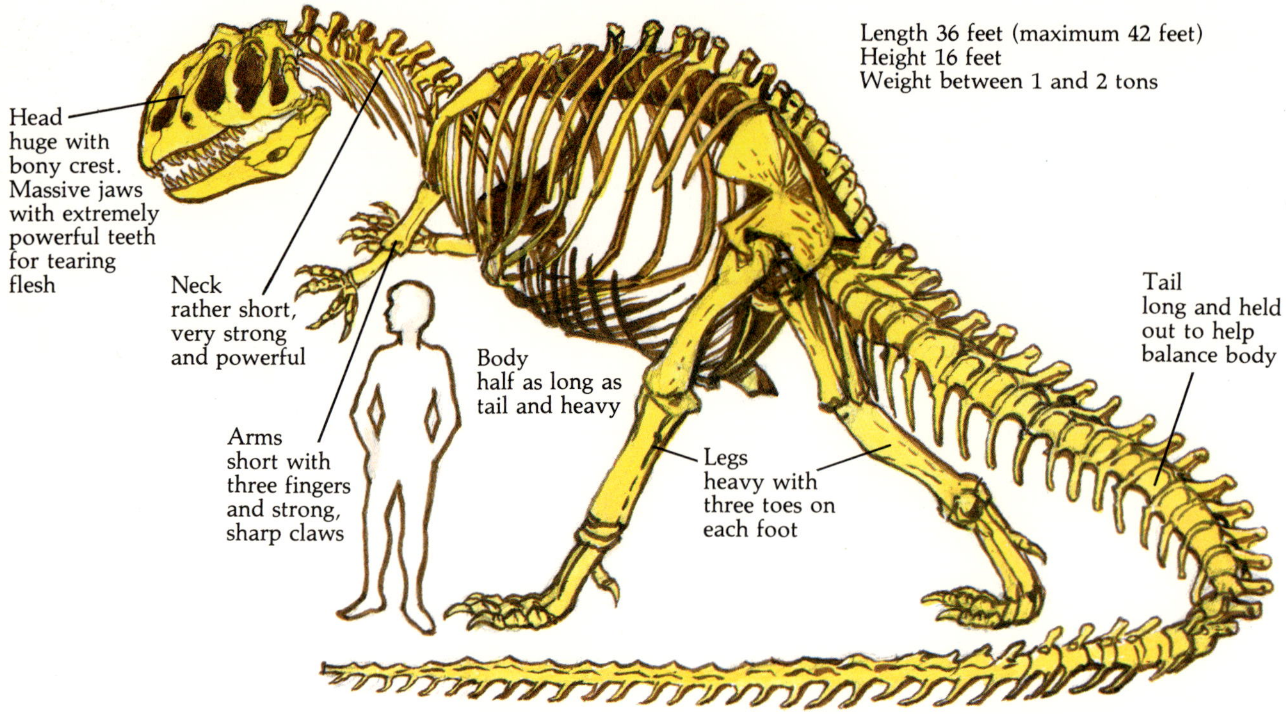

A skeleton of Allosaurus compared to a human form to show differences in size

Allosaurus belonged to a group of dinosaurs called Carnosaurs. The word carnosaur means "flesh-lizard". This tells us that Allosaurus and its relatives fed on meat. It probably did this by killing other animals.

The carnosaurs are divided into many families. Allosaurus belonged to a family called the Allosaurids. They were such vicious creatures that they have earned the title "tigers of the Jurassic age". More than half of the creature's length was made up of its tail. The head was huge and there was a thick neck which the creature could move easily.

The name Allosaurus means "different lizard". This dinosaur had other names including Labrosaurus and Antrodemus.

What size was Allosaurus?

Like all the carnosaurs Allosaurus was an extremely large dinosaur. The average length of one of these creatures was about 36 feet. However, there have been reports of Allosaurus which have measured as much as 42 feet in length. The largest of all the Allosaurus discovered was reckoned to have been 16 feet tall.

Several Allosaurus remains have been found. Scientists have worked out that they would have weighed between 1 and 2 tons.

When did Allosaurus live?

Allosaurus lived in Jurassic times (193-136 million years ago). So far remains of Allosaurus have been found in several parts of the world. These include Australia, Africa and North America. Scientists think that these creatures also lived in Asia as well.

What was Allosaurus like?

Allosaurus was a large dinosaur. The head was very big, and strangely shaped. It had a crest along the nose. As well as this crest, there were also some lumps on the head. No one has yet been able to say why they were there.

How did Allosaurus walk?

Scientists who looked at the remains of Allosaurus were able to tell how it moved. Although the front legs had large talons, useful for holding animals which it caught for food, these legs were not suitable for walking on. Allosaurus walked upright on its hind legs.

What did Allosaurus eat?

Allosaurus was a meat-eating dinosaur. It had to hunt and kill large plant-eating creatures like Diplodocus. To be able to do this, Allosaurus had extremely large teeth and a very big jaw. To help it grip its prey, Allosaurus had three fingers on each of the front legs. At the end of each of the fingers were long, sharp talons.

Although the creatures which Allosaurus attacked for food probably weighed five or more times as much as Allosaurus, its sharp blade-like teeth and talons would help it kill its food. Allosaurus probably hunted in packs.

Scientists are sure that Allosaurus went out hunting for these large creatures. In one case its fossil footprints have been found in the mud of a lagoon. As well as the footprints which Allosaurus left, there were also footprints of the plant-eaters which it was following. Once Allosaurus had caught its food, it could use its sharp dagger-like teeth to tear out the insides. The teeth were then used to tear off large pieces of meat. The jaw of Allosaurus was so large that it could swallow huge chunks of flesh. Not everyone agrees about the food which Allosaurus ate. As we have seen some people thought that the dinosaur stalked and killed its food. However, there are others who think that Allosaurus and its relatives were too large and clumsy for this. They think that these large creatures had to scavange from dead animals.

A small brain

Although dinosaurs like Allosaurus had very large heads, their brains were very small. The skulls were large because they carried massive teeth. The bones which made up the skull were very thin. However there were areas over the eyes which were made of thicker bone. This helped to protect the eyes.

Things to do

Imagine that Allosaurus was alive today. How do you think you would have to look after it, if it was kept in a zoo?

Ask permission to chalk a scale model of Allosaurus on the playground. Or, if you are not able to do this you could perhaps stake out an outline of the dinosaur. You will need some stakes and a lot of string. Stake out the shape of Allosaurus, then put string around the stakes.

See if you can find out how many cars would fit in the Allosaurus outline.

Make an outline picture of one of the scenes from the book. Then color it in using your own imagination. Now cut out shapes of some of the dinosaurs. Color these and add them to your picture.

Find details of the largest animal which is on the earth today. Make scale models of Allosaurus and this creature. Compare them.

All three creatures were flesh-eating dinosaurs. Ceratosaurus was unusual because it had a small horn on its nose. Tyranosaurus was about 39 feet long; Allosaurus was around 36 feet in length and Ceratosaurus was smaller — between 15 and 20 feet